500 Inside Tips for the Long Haul Traveller

To M.N.L.W.

HOLD IT DARLING, PERHAPS WE SHOULD ASK THE WAITER TO BOIL THE WATER FIRST.

A WEXAS PUBLICATION

500 Inside Tips for the Long Haul Traveller

by Richard Harrington

Illustrated by Barry Foley

WEXAS INTERNATIONAL LTD · LONDON

A WEXAS book published by
WEXAS International Ltd,
45 Brompton Road, Knightsbridge,
London SW3 1DE

First published 1982
Reprinted 1983

ISBN 0 905802 01 2

Filmset, printed and bound in Great Britain by
Hazell Watson & Viney Ltd, Aylesbury, Bucks

Contents

Introduction

This book is not for total beginners. It assumes you are already a 'traveller' – someone who avoids conventional package holidays like the plague and probably has some experience of independent travel in the Third World.

This book does not contain all the answers, but it will tell you how to save money and avoid a lot of hassles. All real travel involves some degree of unpredictability, and no travel experience is complete without occasional problems. You could get paranoid about the potential headaches of travel, as many people do. My advice to you is to plan for a trip and execute it with careful preparation – but don't go overboard or you'll take all the enjoyment out of the experience.

Really elementary tips will not be found in this book. What is here is the personal advice of someone who has found out the hard way – travelling the offbeat paths of the globe over the years. These tips are based on experience: they're not the product of an armchair travel writer.

I wrote this book on a trip around the Indian Ocean, travelling to little-known and infrequently visited islands. It you like that kind of travelling too, read this book and take it with you when you head for exotic places.

If you disagree with any of my views in this book, write to me c/o the Publishers. Suggestions for future editions are welcome.

Richard Harrington

Chapter 1

To Your Good Health

GAMMA GLOBULIN AND HEPATITIS

We'll assume you don't head off to the Third World without a gamma globulin shot to improve your resistance to infectious hepatitis. (Hopefully you'll never get serum hepatitis, which has a high mortality rate.)

Hepatitis is now thought to be picked up as readily from infected food as from infected water. You are most at risk on the Indian subcontinent.

Gamma globulin injected with a sterile needle gives some protection for up to 3 months but less each day from date of injection. Renew every 30 days if possible. If you get a booster of gamma globulin along the way, the serum will probably be expensive, assuming you can even get hold of any. Check the expiry date on the box and make sure that the serum has been kept in a fridge. The serum should be transparent, not cloudy, and insist on a *new* needle, even if you have to pay for it. (Serum hepatitis, much more dangerous, is mainly contracted through dirty needles.) If you get hepatitis, see a doctor as fast as possible, and fly home for treatment if you don't feel confident about the local hospital. Travellers have died in some hospitals, not so much from the hepatitis as from the unsanitary conditions prevalent in some Third World medical facilities. As soon as you get symptoms of hepatitis, rest, eat fruit, vegetables and protein foods, and drink plenty of non-alcoholic liquids. If you're wondering how you'll know if you've got it – don't worry. You'll feel sick as hell, completely exhausted and your urine will turn a dark colour. If anyone tells you that gamma globulin injections are a waste of time, note that there is *plenty* of circumstantial evidence that it does offer some protection. So does being in tip-top physical condition all the time, a factor which militates against travelling too cheaply, unless you pay extra attention to diet and exercise.

Finally, the latest news on protection against hepatitis is that a vaccination is now being developed. Protection will be good for one year.

WATER. IS IT SAFE?

Don't believe any hotel personnel who tell you the water provided in jugs in your room is boiled, unless you've seen them boiling it. Almost without exception, even in the best hotels, this water is only filtered and therefore certainly not free of all bacteria. Filtered hotel water is probably safer than the hotel's tap water however. If you want to be really safe, boil the jug water in your room using an aluminium mug and a plug-in portable electric heating element, available from most large appliance stores. Boil for at least 20 minutes. Very few microbes are resistant to this much boiling.

If you don't trust the local water enough to drink it, don't wash your hands in it either, especially if you're likely to be eating with your hands. Keep your mouth shut tight if shaving in risky water and use bottled or boiled water to brush your teeth.

PURIFYING WATER

If you plan to make water drinkable without boiling it, I suggest you use tincture of iodine rather than the commonly available chlorine tablets. Chlorine, if exposed to 100°F of heat for even one day, loses half its potency. Also, it has a shelf life of only two years, and may already have been in the pharmacy that long when you buy it. With tincture of iodine, use five drops per pint of clear water, or ten per pint of cloudy water. (Adding a few drops of lemon juice will improve the taste.) Leave the solution for half an hour before drinking. A half ounce bottle of tincture of iodine will purify about twenty pints of drinking water.

There are many water purification filters available. The best contain a silver as well as a charcoal screen, but no filter will remove all types of microbes. Nor will halozone tablets. The only way to obtain totally safe water is to filter it and then boil it for at least twenty minutes. If in doubt, try to obtain bottled water with a sealed cap, or bottled drinks of reliable provenance and with caps that are definitely factory-sealed.

Drink from a bottle with a straw and avoid glasses that could have been washed in unsafe water. Remember that ice in countries like Nepal, India, Sri Lanka and Bangladesh is probably made from untreated water and can contaminate a safe liquid.

FOOD. IS IT SAFE?

In the tropics, expensive hotels are no guarantee that food is not contaminated. Avoid cold dishes at buffets: the food may well be yesterday's leftovers. Eat salads at your own risk. A cheap *brochette* of meat on a street stall, well-cooked over charcoal while you watch, may be safer than hotel meat left around for flies to settle on it after cooking, or worse still, hotel food reheated after previous cooking.

AVOIDING TRAVELLER'S TUMMY

More traveller's tummy problems arise from overeating than from eating infected food. The problem is compounded by consumption of unusual foods often accompanied by liberal quantities of alcohol. Eat less than you would at home, especially unfamiliar dishes, and give up alcohol totally if you can. It is now the curse of the expatriate, as it was once the curse of the colonial. If you must take a package holiday (outside the mass market destinations, it's not a lot cheaper than travelling independently, whatever you might have heard), take a half board option if there is one. Full board provokes gluttony, and intestinal upsets all too often follow.

PILLS AND INOCULATIONS

Travel agents vary in the degree to which they will help you with vaccination requirements. Apart from the frequently mandatory inoculations (generally cholera and yellow fever), travellers in the tropics should be fully protected against polio, tetanus, typhoid, paratyphoid and malaria, which is now spreading at an alarming rate, and being contracted daily by western travellers overseas. There are several pills available as prophylaxis against malaria. Contact your doctor or the World Health Organization to find out which is recommended for the area you plan to visit, and remember to continue treatment for 30 days after your return home. Malaria is endemic in most tropical countries.

Since smallpox inoculation has ceased to be mandatory for travellers, many health department officials at airports only carry out random checks. This should not be considered a good excuse not to be inoculated against diseases other than smallpox. Regardless of official requirements and the risk of getting caught if you do not conform, inoculation is always in your own best interest.

THE MOSQUITO PROBLEM

Mosquitoes need not be the bane of your tropical nights. If you don't have a mosquito net, there are alternatives. Do not use the light at all in the room you will sleep in. In other rooms use light moderately after sundown. Spray the room with an aerosol fly spray an hour before going to bed. The well known green chemical anti-mosquito coils are effective, as is the Japanese *Fumakilla*, which is almost odourless and works off mains electricity. If these products pose a threat to your concept of clean air for breathing, you can smother your body in various insect repellent lotions, a messy business. Finally there is *Buzz-Off* (also called *Skito-Go*), an American battery-operated device (size of a matchbox) which emits a high pitched noise (scarcely audible) and seems to keep mosquitoes at bay for me. I don't know if it works for everyone. You may find, as a friend of mine did, that if he travelled with his wife, she attracted all the mosquitoes and he was unmolested. Mosquitoes are attracted to perfume, shaving lotion and even the smell of soap so I suggest you leave the perfume at home and use only odourless shaving cream and unscented soap.

THIS IS A HELL OF A TIME TO FIND OUT YOU'RE ALLERGIC TO INSECT REPELLENT.

AIR-CONDITIONING

Air-conditioning in the tropics is a mixed blessing. It is now known that certain disease-carrying microbes thrive in the extractor ducts of air-conditioners. The advantages of a cool night must be weighed against the suffering of an unpleasant illness. You may also wake up with a sore throat if you use an air-conditioner. My advice is that you give the air-conditioner a miss (they frequently do not function anyway, or they make a noise like a train going through the room). Sleep with windows and doors open to create as much of a cooling draught as possible. Sleep naked on top of a clean sheet if it's very, very hot.

EATING TO STAY HEALTHY

The careful traveller can get a good balanced diet of protein, fat and carbohydrate on a fairly low budget. Bread is usually safe to eat everywhere.

AMY.?.... D'YOU REMEMBER WHAT THAT BOOK SAID ABOUT NASTY MICROBES LIVING IN THE AIR CONDITIONING UNITS ?

Brown rice is a reliable source of roughage (fibres) and starch. Charcoal-grilled meats and fish cooked on a spit in front of you, are generally safe to eat and high in protein. For proteins with fat (preferably vegetable not animal), eat yoghurt (or curd in India and Sri Lanka) as milk may not be pasteurized. Cheese is almost invariably safe everywhere. All foods contain some vitamins and minerals, but the traveller should make sure of eating some fresh fruit and vegetables (well cleaned) to round off his diet in this area. Bottled soda water may not be what the doctor ordered for good health, but reputable brands may be the safest bet for liquid in certain places. A fresh young coconut opened in front of you or a whole (not sliced) water melon is a good bet also for a safe source of liquid. Mineral and vitamin supplements should not be necessary with a really balanced diet, but as the traveller can rarely achieve this ideal, take along a supply of multivitamin capsules, mixed mineral tablets and some bioflavonoid tablets. I suggest additionally some halibut liver oil capsules and a jar of vitamin C powder to take in a drink (1 gram daily) for general health (and it's useful taken in larger quantities as an antidote to severe shock; for example, after a car accident where there is loss of blood and secondary shock).

ANTIBIOTICS

Antibiotics have proved a blessing for many westerners travelling in areas where their health is constantly at risk. However antibiotics (*always* finish the course if you start) do have a downside risk. Your body can develop resistance to a particular antibiotic, so the wise traveller packs courses of two different general antibiotics (*tetracycline*, *amoxyl* or *septrin* are the most popular choices) in case he needs to take two separate courses during a trip. Antibiotics may deplete protective intestinal flora, so after a course, one should take plenty of yoghurt or curd or a

WE'RE GOING ON A WORLD TOUR, SO I'LL TAKE TWO OF EVERYTHING YOU'VE GOT!

lactobacillus tablet to help replenish these. Do not, however, take dairy products *with* tetracycline – nor any antacids for that matter. Never take a course of antibiotics unless you're sure you need to.

BASIC MEDICAL KIT

The very basics of a traveller's medical kit should include:

- (i) a course of a broad spectrum antibiotic (e.g. *Septrin*);
- (ii) a course of another broad spectrum antibiotic in case the first is ineffective (try *Amoxyl*);
- (iii) a course of *Streptotriad* for bad stomach upsets;
- (iv) an antibiotic ointment (e.g. *Fucidin*);
- (v) ear drops for earache;
- (vi) antibiotic eyedrops for eye infections;

(vii) an antiseptic powder with antifungal agent to help heal cuts (e.g. *Cicatrin*);
(viii) good old-fashioned *iodine* for cuts;
(ix) a strong pain-killer (e.g. *Ponstan Forte*);
(x) *Disprin* or similar analgesic for headaches, mild pains, etc.;
(xi) *Dramomine* or similar for motion sickness;
(xii) scissors;
(xiii) multi-pack of *Elastoplast*;
(xiv) *Elastoplast roll* (fabric type);
(xv) a sterile gauze bandage;
(xvi) soap

This kit is the *basic* one. See *The Traveller's Handbook* (WEXAS and Heinemann, London, 1982) for a full kit for the traveller.

Chapter 2

Maps – The Good and the Bad

WHERE TO FIND MAPS

Few major western cities have map retail shops stocking a comprehensive range of Third World maps. In fact there are probably not more than thirty such shops in all of Europe and North America. If you have access to such a shop, use it. Getting good maps of many developing countries is often extremely difficult in the country itself. Tourist offices will often supply free maps, but being free, they are generally superficial. Airport shops may stock maps, but these are often pictorial and decorative. Petrol company maps are often good and should be free, but are often sold at

ludicrously high prices, especially in West Africa. However they may be worth the expense. Marine charts are useful for islands and coastal regions. Embassies and high commissions are possible but unlikely map sources.

CAR RENTAL COMPANY MAPS

Maps supplied by car rental companies in developing countries are often inaccurate. You may find also that they only show paved roads. This is so that you won't take their car onto rougher roads, where the vehicle is more likely to suffer undesirable wear and tear. In most places, you're not going to have much in the way of travel experience *until* you get off the major roads, so arm yourself with good maps, preferably before you leave home.

COASTAL CHARTS

If you plan to visit small islands or coastal areas and are having difficulty getting good maps, you could

YOU AND YOUR CHEAP BLOODY COASTAL CHARTS

find marine charts very useful. They are often out of date when it comes to land features like roads and airports, but are otherwise extremely accurate, and essential for thorough island-hopping. British Admiralty charts are probably the best marine series covering the world. Military maps can also be extremely useful and with perseverance you may be able to obtain these through embassies/high commissions, especially if you are mounting an expedition or some kind of official visit which the country in question supports/approves.

Chapter 3

Some Essentials to Pack

SUITCASES AND BACKPACKS

Buy suitcases for durability and lightness, not a smart appearance. The British 'Globetrotter' suitcases, although expensive, are outstanding in this respect. They even look cheap, so are less prone to pilferage at airports than expensive-looking (and often heavy) suitcases. Best of all, travel light with a backpack. This leaves your hands free and you can

I DON'T KNOW WHAT IDIOT SAID A HAVERSACK WAS LIGHTER THAN A SUITCASE.

walk for longer distances with your baggage in a pack, especially in hot climates.

ELECTRICITY ADAPTORS

Don't leave home without an electric plug adaptor kit if you have an electric shaver. There are several compact versions available. You'll probably spend a lot of time using the light bulb part of it. Unless you've got a light beard, don't use a battery shaver. You'll take longer to shave in humid climates and battery shavers may not last the distance. Rechargeable portables are also not much use if you have a thick beard. They don't carry enough charge to remove a really thick growth.

EMERGENCY LIGHTING

Electricity cuts occur frequently in many countries. Always carry a small torch or a candle and matches with you.

LISTEN, IF YOU WANT YOUR OWN ELECTRICITY SUPPLY THEN, TOMORROW ***YOU*** CAN CARRY THE BATTERIES!

FILM FOR YOUR CAMERA

Buy film before you leave home. It will almost always cost more in a less developed country. And get it processed at home – the quality will probably be better. You risk losing the film, however, if you mail it home from the Third World. Give it to someone heading for your country and ask them to mail it there for you, or wait until you get home, if you're not away for more than say six months. However avoid extreme heat and humidity as these factors can damage film, while the latter may encourage the growth of fungus on the film surface.

CLOTHES

If you're travelling rough in hot climates, wear dark clothes. Although they will be hotter, they don't show the dust so quickly. Several layers of thin, loose clothing are best in hot climates since perspiration does not evaporate off the skin so quickly. Wear cottons or other natural fibres – never synthetics.

KEEPING RECORDS

It's useful when travelling to keep a record of vital information and to keep this list separate from your valuables in case they are lost or stolen. Numbers of

AH! NOW I WONDER WHAT ASA SETTING THIS SHOULD HAVE?

traveller's cheques are obviously important but it's a good idea to note the number of your air tickets also, since it may simplify matters if you lose them and have to sign an airline indemnity form before they can be replaced. Remember to mark off traveller's cheques numbers as you cash them. If you lose any, your claim will be more plausible if you can fully document it. Also keep a record of your passport number (and place and date of issue), the place of issue and date (and number if applicable) of any visas in your passport applicable to your trip, your (international) driving licence number, your dates of inoculation against yellow fever, cholera, etc. (as applicable), and for good measure your blood group. Some travellers carry medical information engraved on a disc worn as a bracelet or necklace, in case of emergencies requiring blood transfusion. Your name, your next of kin and their address can also go on such a disc, but precautions taken to this extreme are bordering on the paranoid, unless you're diabetic or epileptic.

Chapter 4

Money Matters

CHANGING MONEY

A common currency fiddle is the Hobson's Choice of exchange that often takes place near borders or airports. It boils down to a situation where you must have local currency and there's only one place to get it – and they know it, and you know it too, pretty fast, when you check the rate of exchange. Here are a couple of examples. You arrive at the airport to pick up the rental car you've reserved. You're planning to pay cash and find that you must pay a deposit – in the local equivalent of $500. You check the rental rates in local currency and they seem reasonable. You know what the exchange rate ought to be, give or take a couple of percent. But when you take your shiny new traveller's cheques to the bank counter opposite, you find there's not much give in the rate, but the take is up to 15% instead of 2%. You go back to the car rental desk and ask them what rate they give on dollar cheques. 'Sorry', they say, 'but we only take local currency, and do you still want the car?' Back you go to the guy at the bank desk, having failed to find any currency touts to haggle with on the way, and you're screwed for 15% on top of $500. (The answer is to always use a credit card or voucher to pay for car rental at airports.)

I experienced a similar situation when I drove from southern Senegal into Gambia. I checked out of Senegal at the frontier post (paying the small requisite bribe, there called a vehicle tax, designed in reality only for commercial vehicles carrying a load). No bribes at the frontier point with Gambia a few miles down the road, and so I blithely drove on a few more miles to the ferry that crosses the Gambia River to Banjul. Well, the ferry desk had it all worked out. They weren't interested in dollars, only local currency. But the fifteen-year-old boy beside me would kindly oblige. His mark-up was a mere 50% of the official rate, and the ferry service didn't run cheap for a car and two passengers. So back to the desk. Would they not take dollars this one time? Sorry, and did I still want to catch the ferry because it was due to leave right now and they were holding it up for me (not surprisingly, as there were only two cars)? Again it was Hobson's Choice and I reluctantly handed over $40 in US currency to pay what should have been nearer $25. Moral: arrive in a country with some local currency. If you must pay over the odds, have enough single dollars, *Deutschmarks* or whatever so that you don't have to change more than is necessary because you only have big bills.

Never change money at borders unless you do so at a border bank in a country where, by law, all banks, hotels, etc. give the same rate of exchange. (This is very rare but is the case, I believe, in Nepal.) Shop around, and always change money at banks or *bureaux de change*. Be on your guard if changing money with a street money changer who has no stall. You could save 5% overall on a long trip by shopping around and on say $5000, that's $250. First ask the bank or money changer if there is a service fee. If there is, that exchange rate may not look so attractive. Hotels usually charge 2% to 5% more than bank rate, but shops may give you the bank rate or better if you're buying something from them. In that case, the rate becomes part of your bartering armoury.

WHERE TO BUY CURRENCY

A country's currency can usually be bought more cheaply in neighbouring countries than in the country itself. Some 'soft' currencies are bought and sold internationally and may be found in Europe and North America (sometimes heavily discounted), if you know where to look for them. The New York currency brokers, Deak Perera, specialize in soft currencies, especially South American money. They also sell packs of small change in various currencies, useful for tipping and paying taxis on arrival. If you arrive armed with some local currency, you may be able to avoid rip-off airport rates and even get a better deal than if you change money in town after arrival.

CURRENCY BLACK MARKETS

Countries where the currency gets too soft develop a black market, euphemistically called the 'free' market. The only advantage to the tourist of the official rate is that if he's prepared to accept it, it's the same everywhere – airport, hotel, town, wherever. A book could be written about dealing in currency on the black market. If you feel rich and you don't want to rip-off a developing country that needs foreign exchange, don't do it. You might also keep yourself out of jail at the same time. International editions of *Newsweek* publish open market and official rates of exchange for about 15 countries with soft currencies. If you do decide to buy at the free rate, do so legally before you enter the country, assuming you can find a bank or dealer trading in the currency you want. The rate won't be as good as the free rate inside the country, but it should be better than the official rate. If you do this, check one thing first. Many countries with soft currency make the export or import of their currency illegal. If you take in such a currency and get caught with it (whether or not you declare it on a currency form), you could be heading for a hard time. The dealing bank that sold the currency might be just as much of a government informer as a street tout offering you a black market deal after arrival in the country. Likewise if you buy the currency in a neighbouring country, especially if large sums are involved, *caveat emptor*.

One of the cheapest places to buy currency (cash, or traveller's cheques in the currency you want if it's a hard one) is often your own country before you leave, not the country where the currency comes from.

BEATING HYPERINFLATION

Some countries have endemic hyperinflation, and if you plan to buy currency for, say, Argentina where the annual inflation rate is over 100%, it pays to buy little by little, as the trend will always be in your favour if your money/traveller's cheques are in a hard currency. In this instance, buying the currency beforehand to get a better rate may work against you. In places with high inflation, it is wise to shop around for the best currency deal as rates will vary considerably. Make sure the notes you are getting are current. Countries with hyperinflation have a tendency to start all over again with new notes every few years, and the old ones may not be worth much as collector's items. If you change a little every other day, you should find that hyperinflation ensures you of a little more local currency each time for one unit of yours.

EXCHANGE CONTROL

Most countries with a thriving currency black market have stiff exchange control formalities for overseas visitors. These usually involve declaration of foreign funds on arrival and departure, and exchange only through authorized agents at the official rate. All transactions must usually be marked on an official form. On exiting, you may be asked to show that you exchanged enough money 'officially' to cover the cost of your visit.

As there is invariably widespread poverty in soft currency countries, your conscience may dictate against any black market exchanges. If you take the risk, be warned that a money changer may be a government informer (the same applies to drug dealers). A few dollar bills, undeclared, may be useful for making small purchases at a black market rate of exchange without actually handling any local currency at all.

CHANGING CURRENCY BACK AGAIN

Beware of leaving a country with too much currency that is worthless outside its country of origin. Exchange back to a hard currency may be legally impossible. Usually, it is limited to the amount you have exchanged from hard currency in the first place, and original exchange receipts are required. Don't count on the airport bank being open when you leave, and expect a rip-off rate of exchange back to hard currency. It's unlikely you'll find a bank counter *after* you've gone through emigration control.

MONEY BY CABLE TRANSFER

In theory, if you want money quickly while travelling, you cable your bank at home and ask them to remit money by cable transfer to a bank of your choice wherever you are. If you think two weeks is fast, that's OK. If you want it any faster, be prepared for disappointment. Your bank is unlikely to have a branch of its own in Ouagadougou. Branches go through associated banks who go through affiliates who go through representative banks and so on. That's already good for a week's delay. However banks make their money by holding on to your money, not by giving it to you. So for every day they delay your money, they're getting a loan *interest free*. If they do this consistently, as a matter of policy, as virtually all banks do, it can add up to a tidy interest-free float for the bank.

That's not much good to you, flat broke, queuing every day at the counter to get your $500 or whatever. The delay is often blamed on a mistake made by the sending bank (never the bank you're calling in at daily, fighting your way through the line of locals). Often a mistake really has been made. The moral is not to use telegraphic transfer of money to really offbeat places. Losing your Amex traveller's cheques in such a place won't bring you much joy either, so if you lose them, try to do so in a major city.

DEPARTURE TAX

Always keep enough local currency aside for airport departure tax, if applicable. Check the rate on arrival and do not rely on the ABC or OAG guides for information on airport taxes, as they are notoriously out-of-date. Many countries do not charge tax for children, but some do, even for infants (e.g. India, Nepal, Maldives). Visas and airport departure taxes can cost a travelling family a lot of money. Often the poorer the country, the higher the rate. However some countries wishing to encourage tourism leave rates low or even abolish them. They may even drop the visa requirement altogether for favoured nations.

BRIBERY

One rule about bribes is that they should never be called bribes. Another rule is that in many countries, bribery is not as common as a lot of your reading might lead you to believe. Like jet lag and Delhi belly, bribery dramas are a favourite of travel writers.

The distinction between a bribe and a tip genuinely does blur in many places. The best distinction may simply be that one you pay before and one after, but that over-simplifies the situation. Some people are more likely to be called on to cough up than others. A lot depends on how you look and on your behaviour. Where there's no doubt at all as to what is wanted, the amount is likely to be very little, maybe anything up to $5, so it could be wise to pay up. Occasionally, but rarely, you might talk your way out of it. More often, the penalty will become more severe as you attempt not to be taken. Never call a bribe a bribe, but whatever you do call it, be upfront about it and bargain if you think the rate is too high.

In Liberia, before the revolution, the police were expected to live off bribes as much as salary. Since most of the locals were either too poor to have ready cash or so rich (and influential) the police wouldn't dare approach them, only the local expatriate community was left to fork out. Stoically, these people came to regard bribes as an extra tax in a country where taxes were low anyway, and salaries for expats. were high, given that Liberia was classed as a hardship post. The blacks of Monrovia are nothing if not funky, and their terminology is worthy of a study in itself. 'Let's harmonize' means 'let's get down to talking business about how much "cool water" you're going to cough up.'

In the Middle East, men secure big contracts by acting as 'commission agents'. In Nigeria, I've seen bribes for government officials written into a multi-million dollar contract in the form of beach houses where the officials would live to supervise the carrying out of the contract. For you, the traveller, the scale is a good deal smaller, but the principle is the same. If, as a bureaucrat, you can make a traveller pay at no risk to your life or your job, then any traveller is fair game. If you're on the paying end of the operation, just make sure you've cleared the way with talk of a fee, a (fast) service charge, a tip, a fixed penalty, a commission or whatever before you actually try to pass on money. Preferably the transaction should be witnessed. Then you minimize the risk of being arrested for attempted bribery, the penalty for which is usually having to pay a bigger bribe.

Bribery may be necessary in some countries when getting flights confirmed or reconfirmed, getting on overbooked flights at airports, and getting visa applications through quickly where application is made *in* a developing country for entry into another developing country. Otherwise, try to avoid bribery at all costs. It could become grounds for arrest in itself.

TRAVELLER'S CHEQUES

Traveller's cheques are great – if you lose them. The trouble is, in years of travelling, I've never lost mine or had them stolen. With most (but not all) types, you pay a flat 1% insurance fee on purchase. When you come to cash them in, rip-offs abound. Exchange margins in the Third World usually vary between 3% (mostly banks) and 15% (mostly hotels in isolated locations). Often (but not usually in S. America) there is a separate rate for bank notes generally about 3% worse than the traveller's cheque rate. This is because of the high cost of insuring cash for evacuation through the bank clearing system. Because of this difference,

HELLO. CITY BANK? I'VE GOT A GREAT OPPORTUNITY FOR YOU TO VINDICATE YOUR ADVERTISING SALES PLATFORM – I'VE LOST MY TRAVELLERS CHEQUES.

traveller's cheques are usually a better financial bet, in spite of the 1% insurance levy, and of course you may just lose them or have them stolen. Most Third World currencies will probably not be available in your own country, but check. If a currency is available, you may be able to buy it far more cheaply at home than when you get to that country, especially if it is a soft currency. Hard currencies, notably European ones, can be bought more cheaply in your home country, whether you purchase cash or traveller's cheques in that currency. Overall, traveller's cheques are still your best bet.

Keep your traveller's cheques receipt and a list of their numbers separate from the cheques themselves and leave a second list of the numbers with a friend at home. Then you'll save yourself a lot of hassle if they are lost or stolen, since you are obliged to document purchase. Note separately the number of each cheque cashed.

If travelling as a couple, purchase joint traveller's cheques. Both of you sign these cheques at time of issue, but either may sign for encashment. Each person should carry a separate list of the numbers of cheques cashed and uncashed.

Always carry some of your traveller's cheques in small denominations (say $5 and $10) for 'topping up' your reserve of local currency without having to cash more than you'll need. Many less developed countries, eager for hard currency, make it difficult to change local money back to hard currency, and you'll probably lose 5% at the very least in the change back. Usually you must show all your official receipts, etc. to prove that you obtained local currency with hard currency in the first place, and did so with an authorized dealer, and not on the black market.

Some countries limit the amount of currency you can convert back to a fixed maximum percentage of the amount changed in the first place.

Chapter 5

Travel Rip-offs

AVOIDING THEFT

Your money, like your camera, is a prime target for theft. Consider keeping your money separate from your passport and other documents so that if you get your money stolen, the rest doesn't go with it. Most petty thieves are not interested in stolen passports.

If you're staying in some place where you don't want to leave your money and passport, and you don't trust the front desk (assuming you're in a hotel), try taping your valuables to the back of a drawer, using silver duct tape. A small roll will travel a long way. But don't forget your valuables when you leave.

Petty theft is endemic in some countries (usually violence is minimal in such places). The consensus is that Bogotá (Colombia) is the worst city in the world for rip-offs. You can guard against the snatch variety by keeping your valuables in a money belt or pouch next to your body and keeping a sleeve buttoned down over your watch. Watch out for thieves operating in pairs. One of the oldest ploys in the book is for an accomplice to attract your attention, loudly and ostentatiously (for example, by trying to sell you something) while the thief empties your bag, wallet, etc. Watch out for *anyone* who could be trying to distract you, especially in busy markets. This is a good reason to avoid street money changers with no stall. Fortunately street theft is usually restricted to towns, and that's usually the last place you'll want to be if you're to see what a country is really like.

REPORTING THEFT

If money or property is stolen, make sure you get a written police statement, or at least a letter from the hotel (if the theft occurred there). It's unlikely the police will help you get the money/property back. They don't usually at home, and they almost never do abroad. But without that letter, your insurance claim might well be turned down. Don't travel without insurance unless you're super-rich and can afford the losses.

CARRYING VALUABLES

It isn't hard to guard against theft. Put zippers on all your pockets or use velcro as the sound of

OH YOU ARE A SILLY DARLING, I TOLD YOU NOT TO TIE YOUR WALLET ROUND YOUR NECK!

opening can serve as an alert. Don't put valuables in back pockets or carry them in bags. Buy a well-made wallet designed to fit onto a strong belt, or use a pouch under your shirt, attached round your neck by a thong reinforced against cutting by a guitar string.

POSTAGE RIP-OFFS

Never post a letter by giving letter plus money for stamps to a hotel clerk or even the guy behind the counter in the post office. Small amounts to you may represent quite a lot for them. Put the stamps on letters yourself and watch to ensure they are *properly* franked. If not franked, or franked improperly, they may be removed later and sold again – the money for the stamps having been pocketed. Needless to say, your letter will not arrive if this happens.

CHAPTER 6

Visas – A Bureaucratic Jungle

BASIC PROBLEMS

Allow plenty of time to get visas. A permit for the Andaman Islands, for example, takes at least three months, a fat 'fee' and countless telexes. Some countries may not have diplomatic representation in your own country. UK residents wishing to visit Mauritania, for example, need to apply through Paris for a visa. Think twice about sending your passport abroad in cases like this. You may well never see it again. Some diplomatic missions make life almost impossible for applicants, e.g. Libya, Nigeria and Gabon in the UK. Some countries simply do not want independent travellers, e.g. Albania and Nigeria.

MULTIPLE RE-ENTRY

Ensure that your visa is valid for multiple entries within a fixed period in case you want to use a country as a hopping off point for another country, and then come back to the first country. For example, many travellers to Nepal travel out *and* back via India, necessitating two entries into India. Most visas are good for one entry unless you specify multiple entries, in which case the fee is usually only slightly more – and getting a multiple entry visa allows you to change your mind. There's obviously no penalty if you enter once only on a multiple entry visa.

JOINT VISAS

Travel on a joint passport with your wife and you can save on visa costs by getting one visa between you for each country. Visas can be expensive, especially if bought in Europe or North America.

PICTURES FOR VISAS

If you're going to need a lot of visas, take a supply of automat photos of yourself with you. You'll need plenty, and it may be difficult and expensive to get photos while on the road.

HOW LONG TO APPLY FOR

When applying for a visa, always apply for the maximum period available, the visa to commence a short time before your anticipated arrival date. This way you allow yourself some flexibility and may avoid the cost and hassles involved in getting an extension.

EXIT VISAS

A lot of travellers are surprised to learn that as tourists they may need an exit visa. Such things are not restricted to Jews trying to emigrate from Russia. A country like Togo in West Africa receives many foreign tourists (mostly German) and requires an exit visa on departure if you stay longer than three days and are not travelling with a tour group. Consider the fact that to get an exit visa, you usually need a tax clearance from the local tax office, amongst other things, and you'll see that it could mean a rapid change in your itinerary.

My flight out of Togo was postponed 24 hours, taking me over the 3 day limit, and I took my chances at the airport without an exit visa from the Togolese government. Fortunately, they knew the flight was delayed or, more likely, didn't know the rules. Anyway, I made it. You can do a lot to bend bureaucracy, but don't abuse this skill or use it to demean the people of a developing country, even officious bureaucrats. I once smuggled a Ghanaian car into Togo. The car wasn't mine, and the only paper to go with the car was a receipt for an insurance payment, but it worked, supported by a sheaf of official-looking papers that had nothing to do with the vehicle.

Don't assume that because you have a visa to get into a country, you don't need one to get out. Check just before you go in. You may even need a *laisser-passer* from the police to move from one district to another, and some regions may be off-limits. Never travel out-of-town (or in-town for that matter) in an LDC (less developed country) without your passport. Road blocks and spot checks help to keep the police, the military and the secret police busy and out of mischief in a good many countries.

ADDING UP THE COST

Visas are usually valid for a certain length of stay, and there is often a date limit for entry into the relevant country. This is usually about 3 months from date of issue of the visa but may be much longer. If the traveller is going to visit a number of countries over a period of months, it may be impractical to get all necessary visas before departure. It may also be impossible to obtain visas for those countries with no diplomatic representation in his own country. (Cape Verde has no British legation – Paris is the nearest). So visas may have to be picked up en route. Visas cost money, but the cheapest and often easiest place to get a visa is in a contiguous country, (especially near much used local border crossing points) provided the two countries are on friendly terms. If you rely on this method to get visas, and it looks as if there could be delays, offer to pay a small service charge 'to speed things up'. Don't ever offer too much or you could end up being held over a barrel (hopefully just figuratively) until you'd paid a lot. In the world of dash, tips and bribery, the rich pay nothing (they have a thing called *influence*), but the not so poor are usually obliged to cough up more than the poor. If you're rich and influential, fine. But if you're not, the poorer you look, the better, as long as you're clean-cut, well-dressed and polite. In some countries, you're automatically a drug-addict or a hippie if your hair is over a certain length. In Penang, if you fitted this description, you used to get SH (Suspected Hippie) stamped in your passport.

Getting visas for some countries is a hassle that stops not far short of torture. (Try getting a tourist visa for Gabon in London, if you don't believe me, or try telling the Nigerian Embassy you want to go to Lagos for a beach holiday in the sun.)

If you buy a visa in your home country, you don't have any choice as to how much you pay for it. Visas can be expensive (especially for some African countries) and as the same visa may vary in price from one country to another (though this is not necessarily so), you can save money by choosing where you buy it. On the other hand it may be hard to find out in advance what a visa for country X would cost in any of half a dozen different places without actually going to those countries to find out.

Chapter 7

Immigration – How to Get By

BASIC HASSLES

Some less developed countries can give you a pretty hard time at the airport immigration desk. Delays are the main hassle, so get off your plane before the pack if you can. If you can't, be patient. There's no point in losing sleep over it. However do avoid Miami Airport in the week before Christmas, when one hour for Immigration and as long as four hours for Customs is not unknown. Most less developed countries require you to fill in a landing card for immigration. You usually need one per passport (there are exceptions – Peru demands one per person), so if children are listed on a parent's passport, just put their names and dates of birth on one form. If you get the form on the plane, that's fine. If you get it on arrival (e.g. in Liberia) then be first in line for immigration by memorizing your passport number, place and date of issue. The briefest of details for place of birth (put country) and address will do, and thus save time. If there's an NCR (no carbon required) copy (e.g. USA), press hard with a ballpoint pen, or you may have to write it all out again on the undercopy.

Some countries require that you show 'sufficient' funds before immigration control will let you through. You may have less money than the country considers desirable. A trick that may work is to carry an American Express (widely recognized) traveller's cheque in Japanese currency for, say, 5000 yen. The theory is that you may fool the immigration official (choose a remote border post if possible) into believing you're rich when he sees the large number written on the traveller's cheque. He probably won't realize there are over 200 yen to the dollar. Better still, carry five 1000 yen cheques. If you need to impress officials with your wealth, the thicker your wad of notes or cheques the better, so in that case you should go for small denominations.

GETTING THROUGH FASTER

Many larger (and some not so large) airports ferry arriving passengers from aircraft to terminal on buses (often a distance of less than 100 yards!). If you want to be first off the bus and into immigration, be last off the plane and onto the bus. It will probably mean standing on the bus (yes, maybe for as long as five minutes) but could save a long wait in the immigration queue.

FORM FILLING

Many Third World landing cards have a 'place to stay' space to fill in. The chances are you don't know where you'll be staying. Don't leave this space blank. Unless you look really impoverished, put the name of the most expensive hotel in town (check a list beforehand). If you haven't got a hotel name, look around and choose one from the hotel advertisements which may well adorn the surrounding walls. Or put *British Embassy* if you know there is one. If you're stuck, smile at the immigration officer and ask his advice for a good place to stay. If you arrive by air in Varanasi from Kathmandu, the immigration officer will be offering to arrange a place for you to stay before you've even reached his desk. Such is business in India today.

Third World bureaucrats love form filling for the same reason that they like uniforms, dark glasses etc. – because they believe it makes them more westernized, as if that were actually something to aspire to. You will find there's a lot of paperwork to get through in some countries, India being the classic example. (It keeps employment down, and encourages higher literacy levels.)

Do not dare to leave a question blank when filling in bureaucratic forms. Even putting 'no answer' may be running a risk. Fill in all blanks without ever being facetious.

For 'occupation', don't put journalist or photographer, even if you are one. Missionary and student may look suspect, too, in some places. If you've got a job that may suggest spying possibilities, put *academic*. Usually the word won't be understood, but if it is, you can always bluff that you're some kind of teacher. Teachers, nurses and doctors are relatively safe professions if you aren't among the lucky few who can put diplomat and prove it with a diplomatic passport.

The longest form I ever had to fill in was a prerequisite for entry to Manyara National Park in Tanzania. If it weren't for the fact that I think it was a disguised market research questionnaire, I would be wondering to this day why the Tanzanian government would need the names and addresses of my parents before letting me in to see the elephants.

SOUTH AFRICA AND ISRAEL

Visas for South Africa and Israel can be tricky if you want to go to say Angola or Iraq at a later date. For either, it's best to have separate removable pages put into your passport by the issuing office before you go. Israel is more accommodating than South Africa, and will issue a visa as a separate document supplied by their embassy. However call the South African Embassy and you'll be given the impression that the problem doesn't exist. Well, it does, and while the South African immigration official may choose not to stamp your passport if you so request (or visa required for UK citizens), it's a safer bet to have a few extra removable pages in your passport. It's worth noting, too, that you may get into Israel with fresh Arab stamps in your passport. South Africa may treat you with suspicion if you have stamps from certain Soviet satellite nations in Africa.

CROSSING BORDERS

Never assume that an exit point from a country is at the border. It might be in a town a couple of days' travel back from the border, and to have to make the trek back if you make this mistake is not a pleasant proposition. Where this happens (mostly in Africa), you may find the next country will check for the exit stamp before letting you in, so don't assume you can jump borders. While it may be feasible, it could also mean a few months in jail or a lot of bribery, or both.

INFLUENCE

The offbeat traveller will often come up with the feeling that it would be useful to have local friends in high places to control the pressure he feels from petty officialdom. One of the best substitutes, if you can't have the real thing, is an official-looking letter, preferably on government paper, signed by an official in the country's government, as senior as possible. The national chief of police is just about the best bet of all, but the important point is that the letter must have an official appearance – lots of stamps and seals. The next best thing is a letter from the country's embassy in your own country. Even if it's signed by the Third Secretary, and refuses to grant you permission to collect samples of frogs in Upper Luganda during the rainy season, it may well impress enough poorly educated Upper Lugandese officials to ease you through times of trouble. At least it could be worth the effort. You can usually tell when an official cannot read because he will examine your passport and other documents studiously, trying to make out he is reading them. The longer he takes, the more illiterate he usually is, unless he's stalling because (i) he's bored, (ii) he wants to show you who's boss, (iii) he's waiting for a little something to speed things up, (iv) he's looking for an Israeli/South African stamp in your passport, (v) he's looking for your last exit or entry stamp. Never show you've spotted that an official cannot read. Illiteracy is one of the biggest problems facing Third World countries, and if you're not prepared to understand such problems, you shouldn't be travelling in such countries in the first place.

INFORMATION DESKS

Many Third World airports have information desks for visitors. These may be unmanned (Madras), rude (Dakar), indifferent (Haiti), helpful (Santa Maria, Azores), or very helpful (Réunion). These desks can be useful for maps, transport and accommodation information. Not all are run by the government or airport authority, as you will find out if you fly into Colombo and are dragged to the tourist information desk that turns out to be run by a local travel company. Maps are usually free at airport information desks.

Chapter 8

The Art of the Air Ticket

TICKETING AND RESERVATIONS

Airline ticketing and airline reservations are two different operations. This is an important distinction. In theory it means that you can make a reservation by phone and not worry about getting your ticket until you reach the airport. In practice, in many less developed countries, the distinction is not observed and you may have problems if you book over the phone and then turn up at the airport one hour before the flight and expect to get your ticket issued at that point. As a rule of thumb, rely on an airline to take a reservation and ticket later only if the airline office taking the reservation has a computer. (Ask them on the phone.) You can always make your own reservation with an airline and then get the ticket issued by a local travel agent.

BASIC TICKETING PROBLEMS

Reconfirming is necessary for international flights outside Europe and North America if you stay more than 72 hours in one place. In practice, it is advisable to reconfirm however short your stay, as airlines with no computer record of your itinerary may assume your stay to be over 72 hours and cancel your reservation if they don't hear from you. Forget the IATA rulebook. It wasn't written with Third World airlines in mind, and though most of them do know the rules, they rarely play by them. Knowing a government minister or a senior executive in the airline may help a lot if they give you a hard time. Throwing the IATA rulebook at them will not. So when there's a lot of pressure for seats, and a lot of money being waved at airlines reservation staff with a *penchant* for the good things in life, you'll be wise not only to reconfirm your outward (or return) flight as soon as possible, but to do it in person, making sure your name is put on the passenger list, preferably with your ticket number against it. Then get the reconfirming office to stamp your ticket as added evidence in case they claim to know nothing about you when you check in. Don't reconfirm by phone with Third World airlines (it's usually OK for European or North American carriers). In the unlikely event that you're lucky enough to get through on the phone, you've got no guarantee that the reconfirmation has found its way into the system. If you reconfirm in person, you probably won't have to pay a bribe. You may have to however if you want to get on a flight that is already really (or purports to be) closed. You may then succeed in 'bumping' an already confirmed passenger. This may seem unethical but is standard practice in many countries, either by bribery or the exertion of influence.

RESERVATION STATUS

An IATA airline ticket has a status box on it. There are three possibilities for the flight shown: 'OK' for confirmed status, 'RQ' for on request, 'WL' for waitlist. 'RQ' means that the flight might or might not be available. Keep in touch with the airline and if the 'RQ' flight comes up 'OK', make sure the airline endorses the ticket with a validation sticker indicating the 'OK' status. Likewise if you're waitlisted and you make 'OK' status. If you get news on the phone that you've gone from 'RQ' or 'WL' to 'OK', do not assume you will get on the flight. If the airline is looking for someone to 'bump' (offload), having overbooked, you may be that person, if you haven't in the meantime had your

WHAT DID THEY MEAN – 'YOUR TICKETS HAVEN'T BEEN ENDORSED'?

ticket endorsed. They'll know your status is 'OK' but, if it suits them, will look hard at your ticket and pretend they know nothing of the 'OK' status confirmed by phone.

Airlines will often ask for a contact phone number (for example, if you've got a flight sector waitlisted or on request), and will assure you they'll contact you if 'OK' status comes up. Some will do so. The majority you won't hear from, so it's up to you to keep contacting them, preferably in person.

THE MISCELLANEOUS CHARGES ORDER

A Miscellaneous Charges Order is a coupon issued by an airline worth the indicated amount in a designated currency in cash or services. Most MCO's are issued by IATA carriers and are usable on any IATA airline. It's a bit like carrying money in the form of a traveller's cheque, though you could have to wait many months to get reimbursed for a lost MCO, and with some Third World carriers, you might never get a refund without the help of a lawyer. All MCO's are limited in value to a maximum of US $280 per MCO unless the MCO is written for a specified flight, in which case there is no limit on the amount. However an MCO is normally written in the currency of the home country of the issuing carrier. If you wish to use this MCO anywhere other than in that country, the MCO would be converted into the currency of the country where it is to be used at the then prevailing rate of exchange (with a percentage on the exchange rate for the converting carrier, which may or may not be a foreign office of the issuing carrier). This means that the value of an MCO, like cash itself, fluctuates daily against other currencies. As with a traveller's cheque, therefore, you are gambling against the future rate of exchange when you buy an MCO.

ALTERATIONS IN YOUR PLANS

Unless you are travelling on a 'fixed date' ticket such as APEX, you may be able to change return dates (or onward dates in the case of multiple flight tickets). Airlines the world over are notorious for not answering telephones, assuming you can even get to a phone. Their offices are closed on weekends and public holidays in most places. They are also not noted for quick service if you visit their offices. To make life easier in case you decide to change your return/onward flight, carry up-to-date photocopies of all the relevant pages from the ABC World Airways Guide (OAG in North America) so that you can plan your own changes, quoting dates and flight numbers. Beware, however, of out of date ABC (OAG) information. Many carriers take months to supply new schedules to the guide publishers, so try to pick up the relevant airline's current timetable (if you can!) on arrival at a foreign airport. Times change frequently; flight numbers less often. Airlines based in temperate zones usually have summer and winter schedules while those in the tropics (especially if operating only locally) usually have only one schedule all year round. Armed with flight information, you'll still have to make phone calls or queue up for hours. But knowing what you want will save a lot of time and hassles if the airline's staff are busy (or pretending to be).

REWRITING A TICKET

If a multiple flight ticket has to be rewritten, this task is theoretically the job of either the carrier which initially issued the ticket (or on whose 'paper the ticket is written' to use the jargon), or the carrier which was to have flown the next sector, if you are changing to another carrier. Increasingly, it is accepted that the ticket can also be rewritten by the carrier you are switching to, since this is the airline which stands to gain most from the change. In practice, getting a long and detailed ticket rewritten in a Third World country is not only difficult, but sometimes impossible, given the complexities of fare recalculation and the low standard of training of airline staff. If possible try to avoid this situation if you do not relish the idea of a nervous breakdown. A lot of work may be involved and some carriers may break IATA rules and find some way of charging you money (often destined for a back pocket) in return for the service.

SAVING MONEY ON TICKETS

Much is written about finding the cheapest air ticket for your purpose. It's true that a little knowledge can save you a lot of money, and that an airline or travel agent will not always steer you to (or even know about) the cheapest fare for your needs. A full fare annual ticket is still the most expensive way to travel, but it can be the best bargain of all if properly utilized, not just because you can switch flights and carriers (not always easy however), but because the mileage allowance fare-fixing system offers you considerable opportunity to stop at various points en route and some slightly off the

direct route at little or no extra cost. A book could be written about how to get full use out of full fare tickets. One word of caution: IATA is no longer quite so generous. If a multi-flight ticket has to be rewritten, there is now a charge for this. Even if no extra miles are involved, the rewriting carrier may now require you to pay the difference between the fare paid and the sum of two separate tickets, one up to the point of rewriting and one from point of rewriting. The sum of the two will almost always be more than the original through fare.

Sometimes it is cheaper to buy two one-way air tickets than a return ticket. The vagaries of currency exchange rates make this possible, so if you do plan to fly somewhere, check using the ABC World Airways Guide whether it would pay to get an outward ticket only as far as the point of turnaround, or a stopover on the itinerary, and buy the rest of the ticket from there. On a long trip with multiple stops, it might even be cheaper to buy tickets in three or more places, taking advantage of exchange rate fluctuations occurring while you are travelling. There are dozens of ways of saving money on air tickets and several American books (listed in *The Traveller's Handbook*, WEXAS and Heinemann, London, 1982) are devoted to this subject.

Travel budgets are usually tight, especially where air fares are concerned. If you want to fly between two Third World countries, remember that flying cost per mile is usually higher for international flights than for domestic flights. It may be less convenient, but you can save money if you fly to the airport nearest the frontier, cross the border by local transport and then fly on again. That way you only pay domestic rates per mile. You may even fly overseas sometimes at low domestic rates if the end destination is technically a part of the metropole – for example, from Calcutta to the Indian territory of the Andaman Islands, which are much closer to Burma than to India.

An airline ticket from A to B can usually be brought in country C. Check if the country you plan to buy in charges a tax on the price of tickets and, if so, buy elsewhere. Costa Rica and New Zealand both charge a percentage on top.

THE ONWARD TICKET

Countries insisting that on arrival you must show adequate means of support also generally require you to show an air ticket out of the country. Sometimes only the onward ticket is required. Such demands may at first seem an expensive proposition if you plan to leave by surface or boat and are on a tight budget. if you are required to show a lot of money, a letter of credit may go a long way.

Usually, the more obscure the place of entry, the less money you can get away with showing. The air ticket, however, is a piece of paper that's wide open for imaginative travel ploys. Maybe you actually plan to leave by air. If you don't, it may seem easiest to fly out of the country to the closest (and cheapest) nearby country, but there you might have the same problem. Or you could buy an air ticket and count on cashing it in later. If you do this, make sure the ticket is fully refundable at any of the airline's offices in the hard currency in which you paid for it. And ensure it's transferable so that if you do decide to use it, you can do so on another carrier if you want to.

However most airline tickets are not all that refundable, especially if they're for short hops. A ticket written in dollars on say Pan Am 'paper' (the airline term for 'ticket stock') ought to be refundable in dollars at any Pan Am office. However such refundability may be overridden in some countries, (those with very soft currencies), by local exchange control regulations, *especially* if the ticket was bought for dollars in some other country. However, if you use an onward ticket to get past immigration in this kind of country, you could always cash it in for local currency at the official rate of exchange, thus using it as a kind of traveller's cheque. Major international carriers will usually not make a deduction when a ticket is cashed in (if the ticket is classed 'refundable'). However some smaller airlines will charge from a little to a lot, and may give you a hard time. Don't be put off by excuses about processing or fall for the 'We'll mail you the refund' ploy. That's the best way to kiss goodbye to your money (though you may make someone happy).

But the real answer to the problem of the exit ticket lies with the MCO (Miscellaneous Charges Order), an airline voucher which can be issued in amounts from US $1 to US $280 (over that and you simply get a second MCO). An IATA carrier's MCO can be traded between carriers, if it is denominated in a hard currency (it is usually in the currency of the country where issued). It may also be valid for any airline services, or usable for a specific flight or flights marked on the MCO, in which case the $280 limit does not apply.

Most immigration officials won't even know the difference between an airline ticket (which it closely resembles) and an MCO with a flight out of their country written on it. They are unlikely to check up on the reservation, which the airline may have insisted on making before putting it on the MCO. This way you satisfy immigration requirements, but now you're wondering what the point of an MCO like this is, compared with an actual refundable ticket for the flight in question. The answer is that there is no point.

If, however, you buy an open MCO, good simply for services worth X amount, you can then travel with a number of separate travel agency or airline letters, each stating that you are booked on flight Y out of country Z. As long as the amount of the MCO covers the cost of the most expensive of these flights, you can then travel into various countries showing the same MCO in each, plus the appropriate letter. Almost always, it will do the trick. If you ensure that all your flights are to nearby countries, you might get by with an MCO for as little as $100, instead of carrying around a whole load of expensive onward tickets.

This system exploits not only the general ignorance about MCO's among both travellers and Third World immigration officials, but also the fact that not many travellers understand that ticketing and reservations are two entirely separate functions. That is how you are able to make a flight reservation on the phone and then get your ticket at the airport on departure. Or why you can make a series of airline reservations round the world and get the airline to put them in writing (even on one piece of paper if necessary) without ever buying a ticket. If they do press you to purchase a ticket, insist on the reservations and say you'll get your local travel agent to write the tickets.

For the same reason, it's also possible to

multiple-book yourself on several flights of different, or even the same, carrier if you're not sure which flight you'll be catching. Airlines don't like this, but they cannot spot it even if they have a computer, provided you make separate calls for each reservation and they don't check to see if you're already booked.

To get back to MCO's. Keep a record of your MCO's number or better still, photocopy it, in case it is lost or stolen. And do the same with your air tickets. They should all be treated like traveller's cheques. If you lose an MCO or air ticket, some airlines will make it difficult for you to get a refund, possibly not before the document has expired (one year from issue) provided no one has used it or cashed it in. If they have, it's your loss. Where you do get a fairly prompt refund (or replacement) in the case of a lost ticket, you will usually be asked to sign an indemnity form guaranteeing to refund the airline should the missing ticket be refunded or cashed in. It's important then to guard your air tickets or MCO just as carefully as your traveller's cheques.

When you are required to have an onward ticket out of a country before you can get in, you may also need an onward ticket to even get a visa for that country. If so, the MCO strategy applies here too.

RECONFIRMATION

If you reconfirm an onward flight by phone in the Third World, (assuming you can get through), you run the risk of believing you're on the flight manifest because your reconfirmation has been acknowledged. Don't count on it. When flights are full out of Kilimanjaro (Tanzania), few independent travellers get into the air until they've paid the unofficial 50 shillings to the local Air Tanzania reservations manager in Arusha. (If you pass that hurdle, beware being hassled by inebriated airport security guards at Kilimanjaro Airport as you try to get some sleep while awaiting your flight delayed a mere 12 hours.)

The lesson is that if you want to reconfirm an onward flight, do so in person. You may be able to do this at the airport on arrival (e.g. in Mauritius), but generally will have to make a trip into town to the airline office. Ensure that the ticket number is noted when you reconfirm, and if possible also have them stamp the relevant ticket coupon. Check that the flight time is still the same, and be as courteous as possible. That way, you're less likely to get 'bumped' if the flight is full. (Confirmed reservations – 'OK' on your ticket – don't mean a great deal once you get out of Europe and North America, although the IATA rules might say the opposite.) Full revenue (i.e. non-promotional) tickets are normally valid a full year, and these days, airfares are likely to go up every few months. The trouble with reconfirming at the airline's office is that they may legitimately ask you to pay any fare increase that's been added since the ticket was issued. If you reconfirm by phone and simply check in, it's unlikely that the check-in clerk at the airport will notice such things or have time to ask you to pay up! But your chance of getting on the flight is better if you've visited the airline office. It is up to you to set your priorities and choose one routine or the other.

No reconfirmation is necessary for APEX tickets. Just as you cannot change your return flight date without penalty, the airline cannot give away the seat it has contracted to sell to you for the specified flight. This is true of all advance purchase tickets on scheduled services.

CURRENCY FLUCTUATIONS

To prevent people getting air tickets cheaply by taking advantage of currency fluctuations and buying with a strong currency in places where the local currency is weak, the airlines periodically bring out currency adjustment tables which, at the time the tables are worked out, make any ticket equally expensive wherever you buy it. The advantage for you in this system is that while currencies change daily, IATA can only bring out adjustments every so often. In a world of wildly fluctuating exchange rates, big savings can be made by knowing this fact. Greece, Egypt, Ireland and the USA have all been popular places for buying tickets cheaply, as was the UK at one time. If you're your own currency expert and happen to be doing a world trip, you can save yourself a lot of money by following the exchange markets on the one hand and the IATA currency adjustment tables on the other. Not a game for the beginner, however, as much skill is required.

A ticket or an MCO is written in a particular currency and if refundable, is a financial instrument with a particular value. Remember that if you do plan to cash in a ticket or MCO for another currency, it will be worth more or less according to the movement of the currency it is written in against the currency it is encashed for.

Chapter 9

Airport Check-in

BASIC PROBLEMS

As every traveller knows, it is very easy to fall foul of airport check-in staff, as flights get delayed, overbooked etc. and tempers get correspondingly frayed. Airport staff are not beyond making life difficult for disgruntled passengers, and have their own forms of revenge, apart from making the awkward customer the first to get bumped (offloaded) if they've overbooked, or the last in line if he or she is flying standby. If you're awkward

WHO WAS THE BLOODY FOOL WHO SAID "*IT'S BETTER TO TRAVEL THAN TO ARRIVE*"?

enough, they may, however, make sure you get on the flight just to get rid of you. If they plan to get even with you for your hostile attitude (which may well simply be a reaction to theirs), they can make sure your luggage gets lost if you plan on checking it right through to destination when there is a change of flight *and* aircraft en route. Lost luggage costs airlines and passengers a lot of money. Much of it is stolen. Most is simply lost through inefficient handling. But a small proportion is deliberately misrouted by irascible check-in staff. The baggage routing is on the labels attached to your luggage at check-in, but only the end destination is shown on your receipts. So make sure the right labels get attached to your luggage and that the routing (hand-written on check in) is accurate. Say you leave London Heathrow for Santa Maria in the Azores via Lisbon. The routing is marked LIS/SMA but your baggage receipt shows only SMA. It may, of course, happen through carelessness or ignorance that your luggage gets labelled LIS only. Or it may happen deliberately. Or it may get marked SMA only and not get on your flight to Lisbon at all. Or it may end up with all kinds of wonderful routings. Check the routing yourself on the labels before the luggage goes down the hatch.

BAGGAGE OVERWEIGHT

While most airlines don't charge for overweight luggage (although they're entitled to), a few do. If you have over the permitted limit and on checking, find that the carrier does charge for overweight, you can avoid paying the extra amount by finding someone with luggage weighing under the limit. If the combined weight of your luggage and theirs averages out at the limit or under, no excess is payable. This is called 'pooling your luggage' and is an extension of the principle that a family's luggage is weighed on the basis of the combined allowances of the family. Most airlines accept the principle of pooling baggage, and some even encourage it.

I DON'T KNOW WHAT YOU'RE COMPLAINING ABOUT, IT ONLY WEIGHS 43 lbs.

You might be surprised at how much hand baggage you can take into the cabin of an aircraft. If you have a lot, put it aside (where it won't be stolen) while you check in. I've got away with 70 pounds of overweight this way, but I wouldn't recommend you try this much if the luggage is bulky. If you do take a lot of luggage on board, stow it well away, preferably under seats, where it won't be a hazard in emergencies. If you travel light, you can even take all your luggage in the plane with you (the *only* way passenger luggage is now taken on some US commuter flights) and save yourself a lot of waiting at the luggage pick-up and Customs on arrival. You can be last on the plane and first off. In theory an IATA airline cannot give away your reserved seat unless you've failed to show up by thirty minutes before departure time. In practice, this is often cut to fifteen minutes, so if you have no baggage to check in, you can save a lot of time at both ends.

HOW TO INFLUENCE PEOPLE

In a standby situation in a Third World country, the western traveller is often at a severe disadvantage if competing with local people who may know/belong to the same tribe as the check-in clerk. If you're male, as well, you are even further handicapped in black Africa if the check-in clerk is a woman. In this situation, there's not a lot you can do, although evidence of power (physical stature and smart clothes) and/or a polite attitude can help. The best thing to at least even your chances with those of the local people (unless bribes are being subtly demanded), is to have an important local with you. Failing that, speaking the local language and carrying a letter in that language from a senior official in the government or the airline may help. What the letter says doesn't matter, assuming the clerk can even read it. Whom it is from is what counts. Having small children (especially babies under two who don't occupy a seat) moves you a few places further up the pecking order. Looking unshaven, poor, long-haired, and wearing jeans and a T-shirt are all guaranteed to send you to the end of the line.

FLIGHT DELAYS

If you arrive late for a flight and the flight is already delayed, you may still be able to get on it if you have no luggage and your seat has not been given to a standby or waitlist passenger (any time between 30 and 10 minutes prior to scheduled departure time). However if you have luggage and it is after the flight's scheduled departure time, baggage handling for the flight may be closed even if the flight is not due to leave for several more hours. Airlines have a nasty habit, devised by their personnel in their own best interests, of usually checking in passengers on time, even if the flight is running several hours late.

So if you call the airline by phone and find the flight is going to leave three hours late, you may still have to check in at the original time and just hang around the airport those extra hours. If you're lucky enough to get a helpful airline employee when you call up (who's even willing to tell you the flight's late at all), ask if you can check-in late and how full the flight is. You may be told late check-in is possible. If the flight is full, however, be there at the original check-in time, whatever you are told.

Chapter 10

Fly Now, Pray Later

YOUR CHANCES OF CRASHING

Your chances of being involved in a plane crash are pretty remote. Driving in a car is a good deal more risky. However, if you are involved in a plane crash, the chances in favour of survival are extremely limited. Civil aviation disasters make news headlines and the thoughts of most air travellers turn readily to the possibility of a crash on take-off, landing or in turbulent weather. If your thoughts do tend to dwell on your chances of survival every time you fly, you

HERE ARE THE KEYS MADAM, IF YOU'RE THAT WORRIED ABOUT THE WINGS MAYBE YOU'D LIKE TO CHECK THEM YOURSELF.

might like to consider that prop planes are considerably more dangerous than jet aircraft. Most modern passenger jet aircraft have a good safety record, with the exception of the DC-10. The Boeing 747 is now statistically the safest passenger jet that has ever flown. However some airlines do a better servicing job on their equipment than others, and some are better than others at pilot training. Among major airlines, Aeroflot has the worst safety record, and the airlines of certain Soviet satellites, flying Russian Ilyushin and Tupolev aircraft, have a particularly bad record. However the accident rate in civil aviation has actually improved considerably per passenger mile flown in the last decade. Qantas, for example, is notable for an outstanding safety record.

If you want to pick your flights according to aircraft type, you'll find that the ABC World Airways Guide lists aircraft type against each flight. These are coded (e.g. HS7 for Hawker Siddeley 748) and can be looked up in the appropriate section of the red volume. (Flight details come in the blue ABC volume.)

Most air crashes are due to pilot error, not aircraft deficiency or faulty servicing. The most common form of pilot error is landing short of the runway.

You may also choose to fly more safely by avoiding certain airports. Among those with a bad record are Delhi, Madeira and Tenerife (the northern not the southern airport). In the USA, Los Angeles is considered by pilots to be the most dangerous major airport. Not many airports have sophisticated radar navigation systems to aid pilots on take-off and landing. Those that do have such systems (mostly European airports) are considerably safer than others. At present, most Third World airports do not have such systems.

Know the aircraft layout of emergency exits. It just may save your life. However, the lifejackets routine is left over from fifty years ago and, as far as I know, there has *never* in the recent history of civil aviation been a crash on water where passengers

"THIS IS YOUR CAPTAIN SPEAKING, WE ARE STARTING OUR DESCENT A LITTLE EARLY, DUE TO THE FAILURE OF OUR ENGINES."...

had time to put their lifebelts on and get out of the aircraft. Old rules die hard.

SHORTENING THE JOURNEY

It may be faster to fly eastward than westward; planes flying in an easterly direction can take advantage of the eastward-moving 'jet stream'. This is why London to New York is usually slower than the reverse journey. However flying eastward and leaving in day time allows you to have more daylight flying time. Conversely, you could fly westward in continual darkness by leaving after nightfall. Flying east gives short nights and flying west gives long nights.

CABIN COMFORT

If you're more than six feet tall, you'll know to your cost how uncomfortable most flights can be outside First Class. Aircraft have a number of emergency exits and here the seats often have more leg room to

create more space in case of emergency. This is true, for example, of the emergency exits on a 'stretched' (250 seats) DC-8.

There are ways of improving your chance of getting extra seats to stretch out on when flights are not full. Boeing 747's are the best choice since you can stretch out fully if you get four centre row seats to yourself. If seats are on a 'free seating' basis, try to get on first and put hand luggage on the seats you wish to claim next to you. If there is a seating allocation for the flight, try to arrive early (check-in usually begins 2 hours before departure time) and get a window seat in the row nearest the rear. If you're told the rear seats are reserved for crew, go for the next available seat from these. Certain crew on long overnight flights like to keep the rear of the plane for themselves so check-in staff try to avoid giving away seats at the rear of the aircraft. Don't be fooled by the 'smoking or non-smoking?' request. Look at the seat plan and actually call the number of the seat you want. Most passengers allow themselves to be guided to the seat the check-in clerk wants to give them. In the back, where the cabin crew sit, you have a better chance of a row to yourself, not to mention better service in the event that the stewards and stewardesses actually turn out to be friendly (an increasingly rare occurrence, unfortunately).

On long overnight flights, you may not get much sleep. By the time the movie has ended, there's usually not much time until breakfast is served. In fact, on long flights, everything seems to be organized for the convenience of the cabin crew rather than the passengers. You can only get blackout eyeshields free in First Class, but if you buy one before you leave home (try a large pharmacy) you'll find it a good cheap investment. A *Don't Disturb* sign is also useful but not always available on a flight. Take along a hotel *Don't Disturb* sign with a pin affixed and attach it conspicuously to your seat when you're trying to sleep. You may even be able to avoid breakfast and get two hours more sleep but this is unlikely as the flight captain will usually blast everyone awake with 'good morning' on the speaker system just before breakfast is served.

The sound of babies crying can keep you awake all night on a long flight. Baby cots are generally situated at bulkheads (frontal partition walls) in modern aircraft. Avoid choosing seats close to bulkheads at time of seat allocation. If your seat is allocated, get on the plane last, after the queue has gone. And if you plan to use pillows and blankets on the flight, get these on boarding as they may be in short supply later on. They're also useful for 'reserving' seats next to you so that you can stretch out later if the flight is not full.

If you have a choice of carriers for a long flight, ring up all of them and ask them how full the flight is that you are interested in. They are often reluctant to give such information away, so be as charming and persuasive as possible. The emptier the flight, the more chance of an empty adjoining seat, and maybe even the ultimate trip – 4 seats in a row on a Boeing 747 – better even than First Class. However a few airlines with Boeing 747 aircraft are known to have armrests which don't fold away. You'll have to find out for yourself which ones. If all things are equal between two or more carriers, instead of tossing a coin to decide on one, phone them both and ask what movie they are showing, if such things matter in your life. Probably one at least will not know the answer, so you can eliminate that one.

IN-FLIGHT DO'S AND DON'TS

For a comfortable flight, eat as little as possible, drink nothing but water (take a flask), loosen all clothing, take your shoes off, wear too much clothing (and peel off layers as you get too hot), and walk up and down frequently to stretch your muscles. Do not drink alcohol, do not eat much airline food, do not watch the movie, do not take sleeping pills or tranquillizers. Do take a good novel that you are already half way through when you get on the plane. Drinking a little water helps to combat the dehydration of pressurized cabins.

REFUELLING STOPS

For many air travellers, there's nothing more disagreeable than a middle-of-the-night stop where everyone has to get off the plane. Even if you're allowed to stay on board, you'll still have to wake up and put up with cleaning people coming on board, unless it's only a refuelling stop. In Dubai, when you have to get off your plane in the middle of the night, you have to go through a security check when you get back on board.

So the number of stops en route may affect your choice of airline. Your travel agent probably won't give you this information unless you insist on it, and neither will the airline if you book with them direct. The blue volume of the ABC World Airways Guide doesn't show stops en route, but you can get this information from the individual airline schedules published in the red ABC companion volume. However not all carriers pay for space in the Guide or are listed here.

In general, the more major a carrier, the fewer

stops it will make. For example, a British Airways 747 will usually stop only twice between London and Hong Kong. Third World carriers tend to make more frequent stops on flights out of Europe, often stopping once or twice in Europe to pick up or offload passengers. In the USA this type of flight with multiple stops is known as a 'milk run'. For those who enjoy a peaceful trip, it is best avoided.

Many major long haul carriers actually use their lack of en route stops as an advertising point if it reduces flying time. And type of aircraft can affect stopovers also.

The long-range Boeing 747 SP can fly non-stop from Los Angeles to Auckland, a flight of around 13 hours. One of the much publicized disadvantages of Concorde is that it must make frequent refuelling stops.

CABIN CREW

There are no foolproof rules for getting service from stewardesses. Some are good, most are bad at their jobs. Stewards tend to be better. There can be few jobs whose incumbents have so risen above themselves. Whether you put it down to jet lag, rude passengers (there are plenty) or that time of the month, you'll find many stewardesses on European, African and South American carriers to be singularly devoted to making your life difficult. US airlines score better on this front, and Asian carriers best of all (especially Thai International, JAL, SIA, Cathay Pacific). In the end, it doesn't really matter all that much, unless you're having a heart attack or the flight is running an hour late and you need to get the pilot to radio ahead to get your connecting flight delayed for you. Then the good stewardess gets a chance to show she really is more than a waitress.

What can you expect a steward/stewardess to do for you in flight, apart from supplying meals, drinks and the name of the in-flight movie? A good stewardess (or steward) should be able to administer simple first aid competently (heart massage and mouth-to-mouth resuscitation, for example); to look up a flight in the ABC World Airways Guide for you (and on some airlines, make a reservation for you on the same or another carrier); to give you details of accommodation and transport at your airport of disembarkation; to supply you with unlimited water, soft drinks or fruit juice on request; to tell you what the next menu will be; to get you aspirins, band aids, reading matter, pillows, blankets on request and without undue delay; to speak at least two languages reasonably on international flights (including her own). All this may seem a lot to ask of stewardesses in a packed Jumbo jet full of screaming children. However some stewardesses have got down to a fine art the ability to seem busy, even on the emptiest of flights.

Chapter 11

Car Rental – The Pros and the Cons

CHOOSING A RENTAL COMPANY

Local rental companies are usually cheaper than the big international companies (Hertz, Avis, Budget, Europcar). However, I reckon the big companies, which are usually franchises, are worth the extra cost since you can make reservations in advance. Confirmation of reservations is usually efficient with Avis, the company I generally use, except for destinations with an endemic shortage of vehicles, e.g. Barbados. Expect great variation in quality of vehicles and service. Top for both in my experience is Réunion, the French *département* in the Indian Ocean.

METHODS OF PAYMENT

Pay by voucher or credit card. Prepaid vouchers, preferably *full value*, are available from the rental companies in most western capitals, or from travel agents. The problem with paying cash is the need for a large deposit, maybe US $500. This may mean signing away traveller's cheques for that amount on arrival, and being refunded in local currency (less the cost of the rental) on departure, with all the attendant exchange problems that this may involve.

CHECKING THE VEHICLE

Always check that the rental car has a fully inflated spare tyre, and an effective jack and lug wrench before you take off.

Make sure all the locks of the rental vehicle are working, and that the boot lock works if there is a separate boot. A locked boot is often the best place for your valuables. If the vehicle is a 5-door one, leave valuables concealed or otherwise hidden, as well as ensuring all doors are locked.

SAVING MONEY

Most car rental companies rent out on a 24-hour basis from time of delivery. So if you arrive in a place in the evening and leave a few days later in the morning, it may pay to order delivery of the vehicle where you are staying the day after your arrival, and use a taxi to get to your accommodation. That way you save a full day's rental. This assumes that taxis are inexpensive and that a full day's rental is chargeable for more than 12 hours' use of the vehicle. Many rental companies have full day rates only, and those with half day rates and/or hourly rates usually ensure that you pay the day rate if the vehicle is retained more than 12 hours. All-in unlimited mileage deals are usually only a good deal if you plan to cover a good many miles in a short space of time. Knowing this, rental companies rarely offer such a deal in less developed countries unless the country happens to be a small island.

A favourite rental company rip-off is to fill the fuel tank until the needle is just on the full mark, and charge for a full tank. The tank is still about a gallon short of fuel when the needle reaches the full mark.

If you're renting a car in a very hot country, consider filling up with fuel early in the morning, while the temperature is still relatively low. Gasoline expands as it heats, and by buying early in the day, you get as much as 5% more fuel than you would at midday for the same cost.

If you want a rental car bigger than the smallest grade, try reserving the smallest if you're travelling in high season. Like hotels, the big car rental companies make a practice of overbooking, and if they've given away the car you ordered, they will usually give you a larger car at the rate for the smaller vehicle. That way you could get the car you wanted at a cheaper rate. If the smaller car *is* available, you might, however, have to take it if no bigger model is available. If you do get a bigger model at the price of a smaller one, remember that you will pay higher petrol costs. With the price of petrol so high in most countries, this becomes a major consideration when choosing a model to rent.

INSURANCE

The big rental companies offer two kinds of insurance. The first covers Third Party accidents and damage to the rental vehicle (though you may be liable for the first so much of any claim). The second insurance covers the driver against damage claims from passengers. Unless you plan on picking up hitchhikers, or feel you're likely to be sued by your wife, this second insurance is unlikely to be a very good idea. Both insurances are usually *very* expensive and I tend only to take the first.

If you do pick up a hitchhiker and you don't have the second insurance, get him to sign a paper saying he will not hold you liable for injuries if an accident occurs.

Chapter 12

Staying Places

TRAVELLING WITHOUT ACCOMMODATION RESERVATIONS

Some people won't go anywhere without prior hotel reservations. I rarely book a place to stay in advance. For one thing, advance booking usually means prepayment and if through the vagaries of travel you don't arrive at the hotel on the day, you lose your money. For another thing, the chances are you'll be booking in advance for a hotel you've never been to before. That's taking a risk, unless you're going to a large chain hotel with uniform standards and you're sure the hotel's location is suitable for your needs. If you do prebook, never prepay via an agent who gives you a voucher to show the hotel. Many hotels throughout the world will not honour agents' vouchers. If you prepay, send a cheque to the hotel or pay the hotel's own office in your home country. The latter's voucher should be acceptable. In practice, most hotels will accept a reservation without prepayment, especially if it is made by telex, thereby suggesting you are a businessman and your credit is good. So never pay in advance, and if possible, do not book in advance. At worst, this policy may cost you a little more for a taxi. If the first hotel you go to is full, try to get this one to book you into another. Show them your business card. (Always have a business card *whatever* you do. It impresses a lot of people most of the time.) If all the hotels are full and you can't get into the YMCA or the local youth hostel, throw yourself at the mercy of the cab driver. At worst, he might let you sleep at his place for the night (for a

consideration). Nine times out of ten you won't have to go this far and you'll have a wide range of accommodation to choose from. Even if space is tight, in the Third World there's almost always someone who will put you up, usually at a price, sometimes for nothing. The world is full of hospitable people, and for many poorer people, it is a privilege to entertain an overseas visitor. If you accept hospitality from such people, do not abuse the privilege. A small present will often be appreciated where money would only give offence.

If you arrive in a village in some Third World country and are desperate for a place to stay, try to find the local school teacher. If that person is male (assuming that you are also), he may offer to put you up or find someone who will, since he is often the only person who speaks English, or possibly French or some other language that may constitute a linguistic point of contact. If the local teacher is a woman, the subordinate position of women in general in most less developed countries will mean that your task is more difficult, unless you are a woman also, or you have a woman in your group.

KEEPING WARM

If it's likely to be at all cold where you're going (and even many tropical places can get cold at 3 a.m.), and you'll be staying in hotels, take a light compact down-filled sleeping bag with you. Otherwise you may get cold in the many cheap places where you can't get extra (or any) blankets to go with the bed you've booked for the night.

Chapter 13

Getting In Touch with Home

MAIL RIP-OFFS

Mail to and from many Third World countries is often stolen en route in the country concerned, usually as it goes through a customs, censorship or drugs check. With most less developed countries, it's a good idea to mail nothing in or out if you can't afford to lose it (and that includes unprocessed films). The countries which seem worst of all for mail theft are Argentina, Peru, Colombia, Zambia, Nigeria, Saudi Arabia and India. International mail theft is growing and even magazines and some letters are vulnerable, as well as parcels. On the whole, airmail is less unreliable than surface mail, but I suggest you use telegrams rather than airmail for really important messages. In any case, airmail to and from some countries can take from 2 to 4 weeks to arrive.

MAIL PICK-UP PROBLEMS

If you've ever hung around waiting for mail to arrive c/o *poste restante* (General Delivery) in some far flung post office, you'll know a lot about the art of being patient. You'll also know that a lot of the time you get the feeling your mail is there but they just cannot find it. And that's often what's happening. Write your first, middle and last names down on a piece of paper, one *under* the other, in clear block capitals, and get the clerk who's looking to check under the first letters of *all three names*.

That letter you expected in Marrakech could be there after all. It might even be under 'M' for 'Mr'.

However, in some countries your chances of ever getting mail c/o *poste restante* are often less than 50/50, so ensure that nothing of value is sent to you c/o a post office.

The safest place to pick up mail is c/o your embassy or consulate, but this is not generally a diplomatic or consular service, so you had better have some strings to pull if you plan to try this one. Your next best bet is an American Express office abroad. In theory, you need to be able to show an Amex card or Amex traveller's cheques. So if you plan to travel with some other kind of traveller's cheque, take a US $5 Amex one along to show at the Amex mail desk. Many Amex offices now insist on a service charge for mail pick-up whether you're a client of theirs or not. A comprehensive list of Amex offices in the Third World is found in *The Traveller's Handbook* (WEXAS and Heinemann, London, 1982) and it's also useful if you lose American Express traveller's cheques.

Don't show up at a mail collection point without an I.D., preferably your passport.

PHONING HOME

If you have to make a long distance phone call home, you may find the only way to do it is to stay in the most expensive hotel in town and wait 12 hours or so in your room. You'll not only have to pay a lot for the room, but also what could be a hefty charge by the hotel on top of the cost of the call. In this situation:

(i) find out first the cost per minute for the call;
(ii) find out if there's a minimum time – usually three minutes;
(iii) find out what the hotel's charge will be;
(iv) call collect if you can;
(v) time the call.

Then there shouldn't be any unpleasant surprises

when you get the bill. It would obviously be cheaper to call from the local exchange, and this can be done easily in some places. However, in other places (e.g. India) the hassle may justify the extra cost at the hotel.

Chapter 14

Attitudes – Understanding the People

BEING WITH PEOPLE

In most Third World countries, the local people you pass on the road are so poor they have never been inside a car. If you are at the wheel, drive slowly. If you have a driver, ask him to do the same. Cars are part of the oneupmanship game overseas as they are at home, and you can seem less patronizing by driving slowly, with the window open, especially through villages. Do not smile and wave indiscriminately, as this can sometimes be condescending, but do so unostentatiously if the situation merits it, for example when a group of local children wave first. Old people will often smile least. Accept that; do not resent it. Drive slowly, look passers-by in the eyes, nod or acknowledge with a small gesture of hand or head, and go at crawling pace when children are playing or crops are being dried on the road. A distinct 'hello' in the local language will go a long way.

Whatever you think of a place, do not run it down to a compatriot if local people are within earshot, even if you feel it is unlikely they understand your language. Body gestures may give away your negative feelings as you speak. Save your complaints for a private place.

RECEIVING AND RETURNING FAVOURS

In many less developed countries, western travellers are asked for their name and home address. Just as the poor often feel privileged to offer hospitality to you, the 'rich', they also feel privileged if they can enter into correspondence with you. My advice is that you give your name and address if it is requested, and return the courtesy by asking for theirs, if they have not already offered it. Write to them if you want to, and reply to them out of courtesy if they write to you. Children, especially, like to have a penfriend overseas and practise their English in this way. Many dream one day of travelling to Europe or North America. If someone has been especially hospitable to you, I suggest you send them a small present from your home country when you get back. It need not be worth much, and it should always be small and sturdy, as it is unlikely, otherwise, to reach its destination.

THANK YOU ALL VERY MUCH FOR YOUR PHOTOS AND ADDRESSES, WE'LL TRY AND WRITE TO YOU ALL.

ASKING QUESTIONS

If you're asking simple questions of local people in many developing countries, especially if there's a language barrier, you may often get the feeling you've been misinformed. Though this can sometimes be deliberate (avoid asking boys aged between 10 and 18), it's often the result of simple misunderstanding. If you're driving a car, and ask how far it is to somewhere, don't expect the answer in miles. Your respondent may never have been in a car and people who walk everywhere don't think in miles. Ask how long it takes to get there and find out if the answer means walking time. Do not ask questions like 'Is this the way to Tamanrasset?' Most respondents, more eager to please than to inform, will answer 'yes' regardless of whether the answer is correct or not. You'll hear 'yes' a lot more than you'll hear 'no' in your dealings with people in the Third World. So put your question in the form of 'Please point to the road to Tamanrasset.' Rarely will you get satisfactory answers from women. Women are underprivileged citizens (by western standards) in most less developed countries. Timidness and fear usually prevail, though the outward signs of these feelings may be apparent disdain or hostility. A western man can relate to a man in a less developed country, given openness, patience and understanding, but he will be hard pressed to establish such a rapport with women of the Third World. That is best left to western women, and is a good reason in itself for travelling with a woman. Travel with small children, too, and you'll have a head start in getting together with the local people.

EXCHANGING GIFTS

If you're wise and travel light, you won't want to burden yourself with too many things to give away as gifts to people you encounter and wish to give something to. A set of colour photos of your house (or your parent's house) might go a long way without taking up much space. Other things you can pick up in city markets on your travels, usually for less than you'd pay at home. I'm thinking of things like nail clippers, hand mirrors, scissors, small writing pads and ballpoint pens (but beware of ink flooding your luggage if the climate is hot). Small things like these often make an acceptable alternative to giving money (except to beggars, which is a whole different subject), especially if you want to thank someone for a service, or for giving you food, or a floor to sleep on for the night. If you're travelling somewhere like India where good cotton clothes are cheap, it's often a good idea to give away your clothes and buy replacements. Getting along with relatively poor people in developing countries has a lot to do with sharing their standards of living without being condescending or patronizing. It also means inviting them to share in some of your simple ways, and almost nothing beats sharing food (the custom of breaking bread with strangers comes to mind here) with people to get along with them, whether you share theirs or they share yours, or you pool your resources. Smile and laugh a lot showing your teeth as much as possible (except in those few countries where this might be regarded as an insult). Local customs vary from country to country and what is acceptable in one place may be offensive in another. This is where your background reading should be useful.

If someone doesn't understand what you say, repeat it, rephrase it, use gestures, but don't raise your voice or get angry. Don't take photographs of people unless you're sure they're used to it and enjoy it. This goes for Polaroid pictures also. If you do take Polaroid photos, give them to the people you photograph. If someone asks you for a copy of a photo you take of them, don't say 'yes' without meaning it. Take their name and address (give them yours; this is normally expected) and send them a copy of the picture once you're home. If you don't want to do this, don't take photographs, or at least say you won't send a picture if someone asks you to. Don't photograph old people or people who clearly aren't too eager to have their picture taken. I personally feel there's nothing like a camera to come between you and your experience of people and places. You're better off with a good memory and no camera at all.

If local people haven't seen cameras much before, don't be amongst the first to corrupt them. Photography is one of the nails in the coffin of any Third World culture.

GETTING HASSLED

In many countries, small boys, and some more adolescent than small, will be the bane of your life, whether they purport to be porters, guides, interpreters or whatever. Surprisingly, it may pay to actually take them on from time to time. Their services are usually inexpensive. Fix a price first (ignore protestations that they don't want any money and are doing it to improve their English) and make sure you choose the biggest and most likeable (every tribe has its natural leaders and that applies to gangs of small boys) who will serve to ward off the others. Better to be hassled by one than by a continual flock of touts and hustlers. Once they get the message that you don't want to spend a lot of money in their uncle's shop or do the regular tourist circuit, you may find a good guide to be a valuable ally and source of information, especially in matters of places to stay and to eat. Someone who keeps trailing and pestering you can turn out, on being hired, to be an interesting human being simply earning a living in the way he knows best.

LANGUAGE BARRIERS

It would be an ambitious traveller who set out to learn to speak the language of every place he intended to visit. You can get by reasonably well on a smattering of a foreign language, and phrasebooks are very useful if they contain a pronunciation guide. But learn the word for *slowly* or you'll find you've asked a question the right way and you can't understand the answer. At the very least, learn twenty words of a language, including how to say *hello*, *please*, *thank you*, *goodbye*, *yes*, *no* and *do you speak English?*, *what is your name?*, *my name is . . .*

BEGGARS

Most developing countries discourage tourists giving money to beggars and point out, rightly, that it is a problem best tackled at government level. Beggars are usually old, crippled or children. The best policy is to politely ignore requests for money. On the other hand, a small gift, or sharing your food with poor local people, without being condescending and offending dignity, can be a gratifying experience for all.

TAXI DRIVERS

Taxi drivers, so the story goes, are inveterate rip-off artists everywhere. Not only is this an exaggeration, it also means a lot of travellers (assuming they are in the bracket that can afford taxis) start from that position and act accordingly, treating taxi drivers with undue suspicion. Once you've sorted out the cost of a trip in advance – if there's no meter – use a taxi driver's local knowledge. Befriend him and you'll learn a lot of basic ground information. Most taxi drivers speak some English and if you speak their language, so much the better. Above all, taxi drivers are knowledgeable if you want to get a feel for the political climate of a place. You could even get advance warning of a revolution ahead. If a taxi driver is good and seems honest, consider signing him up later for a sightseeing trip at an agreed price. In India you can always negotiate a better deal if further business for the driver is assured, as long as you don't mind slaloming along the road between people, carts and holy cows at breakneck speed.

Many taxi drivers aspire to a better job, especially younger ones. A gift of a paperback book you have just finished will be much appreciated. To the driver, it may be an educational textbook in English.

I'M A STUDENT SIR, I'M STUDYING TO BECOME A RACING DRIVER.